While You Wait

While You Wait

Adaobi Ezeadum

TEMPLATE BOOKS®

While You Wait

Adaobi Ezeadum

ISBN: 978-978-978-464-6

Published in Nigeria by
TEMPLATE BOOKS®
(+234)8053506113, 9018279369,
templatebooks@yahoo.com
www.templatebooks.com

All scripture quotations are from the King James Version & New King James Version of the Bible, except otherwise stated.

Contents

Dedication

This work is dedicated to my beautiful girls: Nona, Soby and Tanya. I know you will each grow up to believe you were created enough, whole and complete!

Acknowledgement

PRIMARILY I WANT to thank God, the giver of insights and wisdom. He made it possible. My husband, for his love and support; for being one of the few men who believe that women must be allowed to flourish and bloom.

My siblings, for always so willingly sharing my articles on every social media platform. I have no doubt you guys will help tell the world about this book.

My mom, thank you for always believing in, and giving me a library full of books. It helped me grow and equipped me with the right mindset.

To my friends, Nkiru, Amara (Hony), Adaobi (Twinne), the work you did help me get this work out. Thank you so much for taking the time to edit and make corrections. Indeed you all were my second eyes.

To my late father, you remain a beacon of light and your legacy lives on.

Note from the Author

I AM SO excited to be sharing the nuggets in this book with you. Thank you so much for picking the book and choosing to go on this exciting journey as we discover truths and arsenals needed while in the wait. I believe in you and I am certain you will make wise decisions when the wait is over.

As a single lady, the world is your goldmine, you have no limitations except the ones you set for yourself. You have the capacity to achieve great works once you are ready and you set your mind towards it. I pray the nuggets in this book help you discover how much strength you possess. The idea is to curb the mindset of 'hurrying into a marriage' without discovering purpose or understanding who you are. Marriage is so beautiful but it is better you go in as a purposeful, valuable, and fulfilled woman.

Understand your purpose and you will be confident in who you are in the midst of panic or chaos all around you.

As you flip and read through, may the words in the pages bring meaning and clarity to you.

Introduction

OVER THE YEARS, and given my opportunity to counsel, mentor and coach people (especially women). I have come to understand that most of them entered into marriage with so many expectations but with little or no idea of what purpose means. This is clear from their experiences.

It is said that if the purpose of a thing is not known, abuse is inevitable. When a woman completely puts her expectations on man, she will not only be disappointed but will be easily broken. This is because God has designed us to be completely dependent on Him not 'on man'. You will easily understand that going into marriage with great expectations is not bad but you must accept the truth. The truth is this that those expectations may not be met and if you understand purpose you will readily deal with this and move on not letting it trouble you.

I have also encountered ladies who refused to utilize the 'waiting period', they despise every bit of it and make every effort to hurry through it. While some may be lucky and never regret their decision to get whisked away by their prince charming, a lot of others spend the rest of their lives resenting the choices and regretting the hasty decision they made and now have to live with.

The waiting time generally is tough. This rings through for every phase as it is not peculiar to singlehood alone. I remember getting married and 'waiting' for a year plus for conception. I also remember relocating to a new country and waiting for things to turn around; to land that job, to pass that professional exam, to be fully financially independent and not require government aids. I understand the pains and sometimes uncertainties that come with the waiting period. It can be frustrating and sometimes disappointing but we are assured that all things work together for our good, including the waiting time. Having a clear insight into the truth of the saying that it all works together for your good will calm your heart and give you peace in making sure you build yourself while your waiting lasts. Doing this helps you make impactful decisions, understand purpose and live life to the fullest I believe in you and I pray you enjoy the waiting period.

I pray you make the most precious use of it to fully build and equip yourself for the marital journey ahead.

1ˢᵗ Nugget

ENOUGH

(You Are Enough)

THEY MAY NEVER understand, she thought to herself as she pondered over the experience of what transpired between her girlfriends and her. It was a cool Saturday afternoon, the view from her room window was beautiful. You could see the cherry blossom and the trees with so many beautiful leaves. The cold season was gradually giving way and spring being ushered in. She looked at the clock hanging on the wall and immediately got on her feet. She quickly moved to the closet, picked a beautiful dress suitable for the weather and proceeded to the dressing table. As she sat on the dressing table her thoughts wandered…"how do I explain it to them? How can they understand that I am not arrogant or self-sufficient? Why will they even consider letting someone else treat them like they don't matter?" It all felt out of place.

Every woman must understand that they are truly enough and do not need anyone's validation, she thought. Her friends could not understand this. A gentle knock on the door brought her wandering mind back, her date just arrived. She opened the door and greeted him with a soft peck on the cheek. He handed her a box of chocolate, she smiled as she dropped the box on the table. He took her hands and they both proceeded to the door. It was mostly a quiet ride to the Italian restaurant they had chosen. It was a beautiful place with soft jazz music playing in the background. She smiled as he pulled the chair to help her get in. After a quick review of the menu, she ordered the *Smoked Chicken Quesadillas* as she looked around enjoying the music.

As the food arrived, she tried to calm her thoughts as she began to eat. Some minutes after they began eating, he broke the silence. "Why have you refused to get together with your friends? It's been almost 2 weeks since you hung out with them". She looked up before responding: "They believe I am proud and unreasonable (if I put it that way)", she shrugged her shoulders. "I was simply trying to explain certain key things in life that should be understood 'while we wait' and why there is the need to understand we are enough and do not need anyone's validation to bloom. I was shunned, it was as if a woman's world only had meaning when it revolves around a man. I couldn't understand why a lady must wait for a man before she treats herself to a decent meal. Their ideology towards life is simple: Get a man, make sure he has a lot of money and then make him buy you the most expensive clothes, different brands of hair extensions and cosmetics, get the latest phones and take trips on his account. I really tried to get them to understand that a woman will be limiting herself and doing such great disservice to herself if she believes her life's worth consists only in the abundance of what little penny she gets from a man. I had to withdraw for a while because I wasn't ready to be counted as desperate neither will I let anyone push me into certain lifestyles because I believe I am enough." He listened to her and amidst smiles said to himself, "I got the best."

✳✳✳✳✳✳✳✳✳✳✳✳✳✳✳✳✳✳✳

Often, people misunderstand the term "You are enough". They believe it means one who is self-sufficient on their own, needing no help whatsoever from others. It is sometimes erroneously believed that this belief of being enough is synonymous with being so independent that one need not ask for assistance. Better still, it is assumed that being enough means you are at the top of your game and already have everything about your life all figured out. However, I will like to state that being enough has little or nothing to do with your honest quest to be helped when circumstances demand so.

The term "enough" here is construed to mean 'wholeness and complete' - a state of being where you understand you are who you are meant to be. Thus, it doesn't mean you are perfect or without spots either. I believe understanding you are enough is knowing that although you aren't perfect, you are just perfectly awesome being you, not depending on anyone's validation to do you.

From the fictional story above, the message is simply this; the lady was misunderstood and called arrogant by her friends because she refused to be pressured. She has come to understand of course that not all circumstances and events in life demand your attention. She knows there are certain decisions that should not be rushed and that it's okay to remove yourself from the noise and distractions in other to avoid the unnecessary pressures that jump at you from all corners. At this point, it is safe to assume she would not let herself be pressured into settling for less, and she is ready to damn the consequences no matter whose ox is gored. As a single and fulfilled lady, you must realize you are created, first as an Individual, whole and complete, with a very sound and accurate mind. Everything rightly placed and in conformity with God's standard on why He brought you here. Thus, depending on another person for your "wholeness" may lead you to shortchange yourself. However, if you follow the school of thought that, "It takes someone else's presence in your life to make you whole", it follows then that Jesus as an "unmarried" individual was "incomplete", or Apostle Paul…These men lived fulfilled and complete lives irrespective of their marital status because they first understood they were enough (complete and whole).

This is not suggestive that you should be rude or crude or prideful or "miss-know-all". Being enough makes you understand the need not to be under any pressure to jump into a man's arms and whisk yourself away to marriage simply because you have reached marriageable age. There are lots of grown men and women who haven't discovered themselves or figured out what their purpose in life is.

Being "old enough for marriage" does not just happen because you are advancing in age. There is a place for proper self-awareness and personal development.

Unless you know you are enough you will have conflicting thoughts about your worth! Proverbs 31 is one impactful Scripture that brings to fur how a woman ready to be called a wife should comport herself and a journey through that chapter opens up a lot of immeasurable capabilities of a woman who knows her worth! When you understand you are enough, you won't be reluctant to demand and command some respect, more so, you won't wake up and SETTLE for just anything or anyone.

I have listened to young ladies speak about their

> *Pride, arrogance, self-centered or self-serving is not an off-shoot of this...*

relationships and complain about the 'disrespect' they feel when they are being addressed by their supposed boyfriends' and I always use an analogy to explain the concept of knowing their worth. In my analogy, I try to ask certain questions like this; "What type of women do you think commands respect?" Again, I ask, "If you were Deborah in the bible, do you think men will speak to you in a disrespectful way? What if you were Margret Thatcher or Queen Elizabeth or Oprah or Michelle Obama or any purposeful woman you know at all? You see, my point in all these is this, although I make no excuses for any man who disrespects a woman, it is important you understand the concept of being enough. You understand you are complete and whole and that you are under no obligation to sit around waiting for someone to marry you when he does not respect or regard you. When you truly decide to let go of certain sentiments or limiting thoughts and come to this realization, you will demand your respect and firmly assert your confidence on how to be treated.

When you realize the extent of what you carry, what you possess and how much of a blessing you will be to the

> **When you realize you are enough you will not settle for less!!!**

man that marries you, you will learn to treat yourself with so much respect and carry yourself accordingly. I have come across lots of young ladies who for some reason believe they have to literally stop living because they want to please a man, they give in to any demand he makes and will not dare oppose his ways. This they do in a bid to "secure" his heart and prove they are "loyal" and will remain so, provided they do not lose him. I truly do not see how this helps, rather I see the damaging effect and a resentful future wife. When you realize who you truly are and how whole God made you, you will not stop living your purposeful life just because you want to be called a "Mrs." Engaging in such activity may get you a "husband" but I don't know if you will be fulfilled. Scripture said in Proverbs that your husband will put his confidence in you and he will never be poor! This is enough to make you see how much treasure God dropped inside you. You cannot know what you carry and yet dispose of yourself anyhow! You will not let yourself be messed with or be so gullible to be twisted into marrying anyone! Hear it from me now, marriage is not what you watch in movies, or read in romantic books. IT IS WORK! SOME GOOD WORK!!

Understanding that you are enough helps eradicate that false notion that pressures you into certain lifestyles! You see sometimes we think we need all the material things in the world. We get pressured into certain lifestyles and end up seeking to get funds from 'men' in other to meet and represent certain trends.

I remember when I was still in college, I was not working and was grateful to my parents for the provision and whatever amount they could afford for my upkeep. I lived contented and within the means of the monthly allowance, I received. One faithful cool evening as I was walking home, this beautiful black jeep pulled up a few inches in front of me. The man in the vehicle, after winding down his glass said "hello" as soon as I approached. He asked for directions to someplace. After I gave him the directions, he decided to 'hit' on me. He asked if he could get to know me better and I told him that won't be necessary. At my response, he looked at my hand and said 'you see why you need me because you cannot keep depending on your dad for everything, I can easily change the phone you are holding (Nokia touch), make sure you lack nothing and care for you…boy was I pissed!!! I couldn't let him finish because at that point my patience tank was used up. I looked him in the face and said "It's a pity you think the phone I'm using falls below standard, thanks for offering to even change it, but I am very much content and happy with what my parents can afford and I am grateful. I do not need an expensive phone at the moment, now if you will excuse me". I walked away and was so thrilled I did.

Understanding you are enough breeds confidence because you easily grasp the truth about your self-worth. You get to agree you don't need expensive stuff to be acknowledged or validated. You are not easily swayed or blown away by mundane offers neither are you pressured into accepting certain lifestyle.

> *From the above, it follows that there are actually reasons why people settle for less! Now the question is "why settle for less"?*

If you are reading this book and you still believe you need a man before you start living, well it is time to tell you to stop such thoughts and become as productive as you can before that man comes!!! Anyone that wants to get married definitely needs a man, but till he comes, DON'T SIT THERE WAITING!!! Get up and dust up your self-worth, so it doesn't lose more value. Okay?

Most times, certain factors contribute to ladies settling for less. I have had the opportunity to counsel young women and my findings hover around this reasons…I want you to read the following (culled from my blog on "why settle for less").

Everyone alive is born whole and complete! I say this because a baby does not need therapy! No one gives birth to a child today and tomorrow takes the baby for a therapy session! This simply means we weren't born or created imperfect or "unwhole". Therapy is awesome. There are times I have needed it so bad because I was getting overwhelmed and wasn't liking the person I may become. The reason for this post is simple: I am always at loss for words when people go for less and even when it becomes obviously unreasonable to remain in "this less", they still choose to accept "the less"!

Let's take for instance the case that was shared with me today by a friend. It showed pictures so disturbing (violence and abuse; with permanent knife marks left on the victims face by her "supposed boyfriend"). It doesn't take rocket science to figure that "someone settled for less" in this situation.

Look at it this way; when a person stays in a toxic environment soon the environment rubs off on the person and the toxic nature prevalent in such an environment becomes normal! Listening to a coach a few days ago, she explained how her mom remained in a toxic and abusive relationship. She grew to see abuse as a norm, so to her, it was "normal for a man to beat a woman". Now according to the coach, her mom not only suffered a high degree of abuse but she ended up getting cancer (she had no time to take care of herself or look into her life or go for any checks for early detection and co). Why did I have to paint this picture? It's simply to show that certain people tend to agree that abuse is normal and a functional way to live mostly because of their perceptions and how life has dealt with them.

I know this because of the research work I carried out during my master's program, looking at some side effects of abusive marriages and why mediation is better than the adversary system involved in litigation.

- Most people settle for less because they don't know better.
- Some settle because of the paralyzing effect of fear.

- Some settle because they don't believe they are enough.
- Again, a lot who haven't gone on a voyage of self-discovery settle for less.
- Where a person hasn't understood purpose, they settle for anything!

How can you take steps towards refusing to settle for less?

First, understand you are enough and need no one's validation or permission to be YOU! You are uniquely created - Whole and Complete. You really do not need anyone's negative opinion to thrive. You are smart, fearfully and wonderfully made, so you should learn to get into the act of investing and developing your self-worth.

You can reach out to a mentor and be ready to be teachable. You must learn to refuse negative emotions from past events that try to define your present and tell you that you are less. I want you to get to that point where you no longer see yourself as less or inferior to anyone. This is one principle Job understood even when his skin was nothing to consider as smooth due to the presence of the boils and all manner of infirmity he was dealt with. He rightly made his friends realize this truth when he spoke to them during their conversations as recorded in the book of Job, he said: **"What you know I know, I am not inferior to you"**.

You must digest this truth and refuse to be treated less. The reason I say this is because there are certain things that may happen in life or certain situations you may find yourself in that will open up doors for friends to advise you or tell you what to do. The situation may even present itself while you wait, but you must be determined to see yourself as "worth it", not "worthless". And you must refuse certain counsels targeted at bringing you down or fashioned to make you feel less and inferior.

You also need to understand that you have been given all that pertains to life and godliness. If your heavenly Father created you any less that you should live like you weren't enough, He would not have sent His son to die for you and me. So go on and live life with this sense that although you aren't perfect, a perfect God sent His son to die for you. This means you are ENOUGH so that even if you were the only being on earth, you are still "enough" to be died for. Don't let anyone steal this truth from you. You are no less than anyone who deserves a good life, neither are you lesser than anyone who refuses to be disrespected and bullied into thinking they are not enough.

2ⁿᵈ Nugget

DISCOVER

(Discover Who You Are)

ACCORDING TO THE dictionary, "discover" means to see, get knowledge of, learn of, find, or find out; gain sight or knowledge of (something previously unseen or unknown). The nuggets in these pages are so important because an honest inward search and the truth you find out from this discovery have the capability of moving you from point A to point B. **WHO ARE YOU?** (You really need to answer this question). I remember getting a message notification on one of my social media inbox from a pretty young lady. Her plea was simple yet carried great weight. She was over 22years old and what she wrote was this;

"Please ma, I do not know my worth or value, I also do not know how to face my fears, can you please help me?"

I read her message and responded almost immediately! Listen, until you take a deliberate and intentional decision to discover who you truly are (much as it's a continuous process) you will have great difficulty navigating through these core human make-ups. **"Worth and Value"**. Why is it paramount to know and understand what your worth and value is? This is simply because it is the value you place on yourself that people respond to especially with regards to the ways they treat you. No one will value you or respect you above the value and respect you place on yourself. That is why you must be so deliberate and intentional about knowing and understanding your worth and value. If you do not know this (your worth and value), why then do you want to get married?

Now, as a single woman, you need to take time to do some deep thinking and discover "who you are"? If you don't know who you are, you will settle for just anything or anyone!

If you have discovered yourself and you know where you are going, his silly sexual advances should be the last worry you have. Those very empty talks about wanting to have sex with you before marriage will even make you laugh and happily tell him "boy bye".

I understood not only who I was but whose I was as well. So there were talks that were just simply foolish and unimportant to waste valuable time on. When you have discovered yourself, you will know what triggers you and what weakens you; you will equally know what propels you and makes you advance. Again when you have discovered who you are, you will easily agree with me that not everything matters. You will not be easily swayed simply because you want to meet up with the Joneses. Life will be very meaningful and you will wake up living every day as intentionally as possible, making every hour count with the determination to let your life be as impactful as ever.

No one who has discovered their true self sits still in life waiting for hand me downs and crumbs from the table. As a lady in the wait, you cannot relax waiting for a "marriage" when there are a million and one things to do. When the realization of who we are comes to us, we will do mighty works greater than that exhibited by the proverbs 31 woman.

The Voyage Of Self-Discovery

Most times some of these concepts seem quite vague to the mind. I can imagine someone asking, "Voyage of self-discovery" what exactly does that mean? I know me, I know what my name is, and who my parents are (foster/adoptive), possibly where my root stems from etc. So what discoveries are we actually talking about? Self-discovery or self-awareness is actually one of the most important aspects of "YOU"! Various authors have given insights into what this concept means. However, according to the American English Dictionary definition, self-discovery means "becoming aware of one's true potential, character, motives, etc.

I remember the first time this became clear to me! I was like "wow!!!" This concept should have been explained to me while I was still in junior high, maybe I would have developed myself so well so early in life and of course, birthed mind-blowing unicorn ideas (winks). So what is the point? Once a person becomes aware of their full potential, there is no stopping you. I was privileged to coach a lot of young undergraduate students back then while in college. For every session we had it seemed scales fell off because until they realized they were living below their potential they were slaves to "many things".

Now how will you feel when you know as a matter of fact you have 1 million US dollars sitting in your account? I mean you can walk into any shop and buy the best items you desire just the way you desire it, right? Because you are so sure of what you have - THE MONEY IN YOUR ACCOUNT. Now place this analogy next to "potential". How will you carry yourself when you truly discover what your worth is and what you are capable of achieving? As an honest statement of fact, if you "discover yourself" the confidence it gives will birth a million dollars over and over because you no longer wait for hand me downs (crumbs). Others rather come to your table for "hand me downs".

When you become aware of who you truly are, you will not settle for just anything or anyone, you will be so deliberate and intentional about decisions you make and actions you take, and you will rather focus on what matters because truly not everything matters. Being aware of yourself places you above certain life dramas.

I remember when my dad will say "It's not every word you should respond to." This is equally right in this circumstance when you realize who you are, it's not everything that should attract you neither is it everything you should attract.

Why is it crucial to "discover oneself"?

1.   A greater percentage of the value you place on yourself is determined by how well you know yourself. Hear me, no one will perceive you higher than the value you place on yourself. A lot of people do not know this, and so settle for anything even in relationships/career, etc.

2   Until you have fully discovered and become aware of yourself, forming opinions and standing firm on them will be a struggle and anyone can easily twist your mind and sell their own ideas to you.

3   It's paramount to discover oneself because this makes your life less complicated especially in the area of making choices!

How can you take steps towards self-discovery?

• We are created as spiritual beings, so we first seek a connection with God.

• Invest in your "personal development"!!! This is so important.

• Have a sense of purpose and be clear about what you want in life.

• Ask yourself who am I? It may sound simple, but it can be effective. Who are you? What brings you joy? What are you most afraid of? What feelings are leading you right now?

• Find your core values. Your core values drive you. They help define who you are and who you aim to be. Use this tool to help you find your core values. (Creativity, equality, understanding, intellectual status, and family-orientedness are among the common personal values listed).

• See challenges, not struggles. When we struggle, we often lose touch with ourselves. We feel lost. One way to counteract this is to see struggles as challenges.

• Surround yourself with people who allow you to grow. The journey of self-discovery is not a solo one, although it may feel like that at times. If you are surrounded by people who do not have your best interests at heart, then you are will not be able to grow into the best possible version of yourself. Eliminate those people from your life, and surround yourself with people who allow you to grow.

As Eleanor Roosevelt said, "Friendship with oneself is all important because without it one cannot be friends with anyone else in the world." Journaling helps us figure out who we are, what we need and what we want. It can help us make better decisions and focus on the very things that support us in taking compassionate care of ourselves and others.

Here are prompts, questions, and ideas to explore in your journal to get to know yourself better.

1. My favorite way to spend the day is…
2. If I could talk to my teenage self, the one thing I would say is…
3. The two moments I'll never forget in my life are… *Describe them in great detail, and what makes them so unforgettable.*
4. Make a list of 30 things that make you smile.
5. The words I would like to live by are…
6. I couldn't imagine living without…
7. When I'm in pain — physical or emotional — the kindest thing I can do for myself is…
8. Make a list of the people in your life who genuinely support you, and who you can

genuinely trust. (Then make time to hang out with them.)

9. What does unconditional love look like for you?

10. What would you do if you loved yourself unconditionally? How can you act on these things whether you do or don't?

11. I really wish others knew about me…

12. Name what is enough for you.

13. If my body could talk, it would say…

14. Name a compassionate way you've supported a friend recently. Then write down how you can do the same for yourself.

15. What do you love about life?

16. What always brings tears to your eyes? (As Paulo Coelho has said, "Tears are words that need to be written.")

17. "Write about a time when work felt real to you, necessary and satisfying. Paid or unpaid, professional or domestic, physical or mental." (Also a prompt from Abercrombie's kicking in the Wall.)

18. Write about your first love — whether a person, place or thing.

19. Using 10 words, describe yourself.

20. What's surprised you the most about your life or life in general?

21. What can you learn from your biggest mistakes?

22. I feel most energized when…
23. "Write a list of questions to which you urgently need answers." (This is probably my favorite prompt from Abercrombie's book.)
24. Make a list of everything that inspires you — from books to web sites to quotes to people to paintings to stores to the stars.
25. What's one topic you need to learn more about to help you live a more fulfilling life? (Then learn about it.)
26. I feel the happiest in my skin when…
27. Make a list of everything you'd like to say no to.
28. Make a list of everything you'd like to say yes to.
29. Write the words you need to hear (like affirmations).

Be Self-Aware

What does this mean?

Conscious knowledge of one's own character, feelings, motives, and desires. Having a clear perception of your personality, including strengths, weaknesses, thoughts, beliefs, motivation, and emotions. Self-Awareness allows you to understand other people, how they perceive you, your attitude and your responses to them at the moment.

If you are not self-aware, how then can you know what perception tallies with yours? As a Christian, you ought to know your place as God's child too!!! BE VERY AWARE OF THAT!!!

Be emotionally intelligent. This is one attribute you will be needing definitely both in marriage and in every area of your life. Emotional Intelligence – EQ or EI is:

A term created by two researchers – Peter Salavoy and John Mayer – and popularized by Dan Goleman in his 1996 book of the same name. We define EI or EQ as the ability to:

- Recognize, understand and manage our own emotions.
- Recognize, understand and influence the emotions of others.

In practical terms, this means being aware that emotions can drive our behavior and impact people (positively and negatively), and learning how to **manage those emotions** – both our own and others – especially when we a under pressure.

So for you to be self-aware. You must learn what your emotions are and how to handle it.

Also, in discovery, you deal with your **fears**. You must understand fear is a strong force that can shut you down if you don't address it. Read the insightful write up below culled from my blog, this will further explain the concept of fear:

HELLO FEAR

March 14, 2019

Hello, my name is Fear!

Waking up at exactly 2:43 am on a Thursday morning, the room was covered in total darkness, she immediately felt a sense of fear. Fear so real that she thought she could hold it with her bare hands. All her being cringed in fear, in this state she could easily believe and process any negative thoughts that drop in her mind because fear is present and has unleashed its paralyzing effect on her. But there was something she didn't know, she didn't know that her room was no different a few hours ago before she went to bed, she didn't know she could exercise power over fear if she just braced up, walked towards the light and switched it on...I mean how easier could that be right? But hey, Fear was present and did its work (paralyzed her and got her into thinking about the unknown). This fictional picture I painted may resonate more with kids, but there are lots of grown folk who have not come to realize that "fear thrives in the unknown". One of the many factors that hinder a person from discovering their true self and unleashing their potentials is Fear.

Fear has such a negative force and its effect can be overwhelmingly dangerous! Don't get it wrong, fear is a natural survival human instinct and may not be completely negative or bad. It ultimately depends on what message it communicates to you at that particular point in time. For instance, if the communication is to keep you alert, active and focused, then it's good but if it rubs you of your sense of thought, then negative fear has taken over and can never produce any positive impact.

In this article, I am discussing the negative effects of fear.

I believe everyone born alive has experienced fear in one form or the other. I remember when I was so paralyzed by fear as I headed home from college after my lectures. There was a little bush by the pedestrian walkway leading to my house (it's a short cut and saves you a whole lot of hours taking the main route home). As I walked, a green snake suddenly crawled speedily across to the other side of the road (green grasses). Let's say it happened 10 feets away from where I was, but the fearful impact it had on me was exceedingly great! I stood there for over 20mins in a somewhat frozen state!

Not sure if I ever wanted to move forward or if I should just turn back and embark on a second missionary via the main route. Part of me felt the snake will come right out and bite me if I dare moved. Still, in my frozen state, my neighbor came out from their gate and saw me standing like a statute. Now did I mention that this incident happened less than 30 feet to my house (I could see where I was going but fear would not let me take another step forward)

He called out and looking up I asked him if he could come get me because I just saw a snake and not sure if I can take further steps. He laughed and came over. Phew, what a relief, as soon as he approached I refused to walk, I actually run-walked (if I may borrow such English).

What lesson can you learn from my experience? For one I understood firsthand how fear can hinder "planned progress".

Negative Impact

How does fear negatively impact on your journey to self-discovery?

Discovering your true self and placing value on your worth will be a struggle if you are not able to face your fears or ask for help when dealing with it. Negative fear will not only tamper with your self-discovery it will keep you at a mediocre state.

A lot of times I see people giving up on their dreams because they fear what the outcome may be. Most individuals have ended up marrying someone they were not compatible with because they feared the unknown (what if no one comes for me again). Others remain in abusive relationships enduring heart-breaking nightmares just mostly because they fear what people will say or what their family will think or how the society will label and stigmatize them. Fear can negatively affect your journey in a plethora of ways: (this list is only a sneak peek into what fear does. It is in no way exhaustive:

- It takes away your sense of reasoning and keeps you in a moronic state.
- It gives you no sense of worth making you believe you are less.
- It constantly makes you underperform.
- It makes you gullible to accept others negative opinions of you.
- It hinders the starting or accomplishment of projects.
- Fear makes you susceptible to intense reactions and impulse reactions.
- It can weaken the creation of long-term memories and damage the part of the brain that helps in making this possible (the hippocampus), short circuiting the response paths and causing constant feelings of anxiety. (My research work on effects of PSTD and fear).

How can you avoid the negative impact of fear?

(Just sharing 3 points)

Depending on your faith or belief, I come from a place where I have been taught that God has not given us a spirit of fear, but of a sound mind and boldness. So it's trite to say it's very paramount to connect to God when fear looms. Pick your spiritual book and draw strength from it. You can equally mediate. The focal point is to connect to something (a force stronger than you that can help you reset your mind and overcome fear.)

Learn to increase your positive emotions. Because fear causes us to remember negative events. It's our duty to be deliberate and intentional in working on only noticing positive emotions or creating one. According to research by Barbara Fredrickson, positivity broadens our perspective— we literally have a wider view, which offers us more options. And the more we practice positivity, the more it builds, creating a resilience that allows us to function even in difficult times.

Find your life's purpose. If you know why you are here you are more likely to keep pushing forward in fulfillment of your life purpose. Fear will not stop you because everyone who has figured out their life's purpose, knows fear will not stop them even though our purpose can be overwhelmingly big and cause us to shudder.

Does waiting seem endless?

When you begin to realize who you are and your worth, certain things gradually fall into place. I remember when I just accepted Christ into my life at age 16 and started reading the Scriptures. It was such an amazing experience discovering myself in the Lord! Wow! I became so intentionally about how I lived, what I did, what I said because I knew whose I was! Life wasn't supposed to be lived anyhow anymore, because I was discovering another dimension of myself that carried greater worth! You can be sure to experience these changes when you realize who you are so you are fully fortified and have no doubt about who you are, and waiting still seems endless then MOVE!

There are times you may flip the coin to get to your destination. Going through the book of Ruth, she is one of the people in Scripture I refer to as the "Game Changers". Ruth made moves, one of which brought an end to her "waiting era" and ushered in Boaz, her kinsman-redeemer. (Read the whole of Ruth chapter 3).

You are ready to be married, what are you doing to see it materializes? If you prefer to settle with a pastor you prayed about this and have a positive affirmation in your spirit, then get to work. Attend meetings, conferences, workshops, symposiums, engagements, outings, etc. that will bring this sought of mind together! When you are there make yourself seen, this is not suggestive of the fact that you be immoral, lose or playing a "wife" role…You can be seen when you exhibit wisdom, knowledge, understanding, and skill because you are an asset to the nation and a carrier of immeasurable value.

I remember when I attended a conference at Kofo Abayomi, Victoria Island, Lagos, Nigeria. I WAS SEEN! I got numerous contacts and "lots of interested persons"... This is just an example, have you gone to a gathering and a lady just stands out? You admire her not because she's wearing the best dress, but because whenever they held the mic to speak, everyone wanted to listen to her. I can relate so well! And it doesn't happen overnight! It takes its process, based on the books you read or the minds you choose to rob yours with, and the person you have made God be to you through the help of the spirit.

Take care of yourself

Ruth not only washed and dressed well, but Scripture said she also "smelled nice". Understand the power of good hygiene while you wait. This personally has nothing to do with makeup (if you need to apply them please do) but as a single lady the last thing I worried about was to make up (my friends can attest to that). I will use that money to buy books that I will read or look for a conference to attend, because I felt the time for make-up would come and boy am rubbing it now! But the point is this, YOU MUST LOOK GOOD AND SMELL NICE.

3rd Nugget

GOD

Grow in Your knowledge of Him

WHO IS GOD to you? How much worth do you place on Him? Do you know him for yourself? Have you continually worked and improved your relationship with Him? **Really who is God to you?**

Let me share this story: As a young girl, she always fantasized about what her wedding day will look like. She also believed marriage will play out just exactly as the Disney princess, happy ending fairy tale cartoons always painted love and romance. She met her prince charming, what seemed like a perfect ending love affair kicked off and soon engagement announcements filled the air… everyone was happy for them. They were happy it seemed but she may not go on with the engagement plans. Prince Charming was going to cause her great trouble (both mentally, emotionally and physically if she continued). She knew it was time to retreat and of course, she went back to God.

Now the truth is that we may make mistakes, however not knowing God or having a relationship with Him is a dangerous place to be. From the story above the young girl understood that going on with the relationship spelled doom for her. At that moment going back to God becomes the best option. She was able to do this because she knew Him.

Do you know Him? Who and what does God represent to you? You cannot actually live to navigate through life without building and developing a relationship with Him. Till you grow in the knowledge of Him certain decisions will be tough and avoiding certain wrong decisions may be extremely difficult. If you desire to be married understand that working out your marriage in most circumstances depends on how much God you have.

I have been married for a while and I know for a fact that there are certain situations I resolved in the place of prayer. A lot of instances abound. I remember when I had to pray over certain issues I no longer have to worry about today. There are others I still pray about and the rest I resolve with wisdom and common sense.

You see, I have heard people say but there are non-Christians who live well so why does this matter, why does knowing God personally have to be something to worry about? News flash: Christians have been promised trials and wonderful troubles, so you don't want to compare yourself with those who aren't going to have troubles...Jesus said in this world you will have trials and tribulations and all sorts (in this Life, and marriage is part of your journey) but the amazing thing is that we will come out unharmed! But you will most likely be harmed if you don't know him or know this. If you don't know him personally, you personally miss out on a lot. I have had some say most good women marry and end up being beaten or being cheated on etc... as sad as this reality is, I personally cannot judge other women's stories. I can only judge mine, and I can attest that God has proved true. This doesn't mean we don't have temptations or normal partner issues but we are deliberate and intentional on respect and support.

If you know God and understand how he speaks with you, I don't know how you will end up wrongly. I believe when we know God for ourselves we are able to discern certain dangerous pitfalls, especially in this area of choosing who to spend your life with. This is where putting God in your relationship comes in, try as much as possible to keep to the tenets of a Godly courtship and refuse to compromise on certain fundamental foundations. Love God! I know the waiting time can be tough, but if you can just use this time to be crazy about God! Love him recklessly, love him madly, and be mercilessly in love with him, fall in love with him over and over again, put him at the center of your life. God is faithful; He is a rewarder (be diligent and see if He won't reward you).

Don't let the world set standards for your relationship. Have boundaries, have core values and refuse to compromise on them. This becomes relatively easy when you have heard it before and am saying it again. Don't break God's principles on sex and morality because a man believes you should! Always choose God's word above "mere men". You are God's masterpiece and it's to our own advantage to trust that He is able, even when it doesn't make any sense. His faithfulness will prove to you that indeed ALL THINGS WORK TOGETHER FOR GOOD (INCLUDING THIS WAITING PERIOD). The most important thing is to know to have a relationship with God. I know we make mistakes, we fail, we fall… but we don't remain down, we may have it missed it and compromised but here is the amazing truth about God. His mercy always speaks for us. He loves you regardless you have discovered who you are. While you wait, God wishes you open up to Him in every possible issue of concern regarding your waiting period.

He wants you to be so free with Him that you get to that point where He becomes the center of your life. He wants to be deeply connected with you to the extent he freely gives you a clue on every possible person having an interest in you. He is that caring and can be so detailed and interested in every aspect of our life.

Knowing God for yourself: Why this is paramount?

First of all, all life in being depends on Him, including yours! Knowing God for oneself is so crucial because certain life events have been designed in such a way that sole dependency on God (a greater force is necessary to be able to navigate through certain troubled turbulent waters.

I remember listening to a young lady once who was worried sick and really distressed on the issue of which suitor was right. Her dilemma started after the 'prayer people' got involved. She was asked to get the pictures of the young men so prayers could be made to help her get closure and make an accurate decision. Now, there is nothing wrong with seeking counsel or asking people to join you in praying for specific needs. But there is every necessity in being spiritually alert yourself. It is paramount to grow in faith and get to know God for yourself. It makes this phase less complicated and reduces the noise and intrusion from others.

When you have grown to know God for yourself personally, He will direct your path. You will be less inclined to run to people for solution. You will no longer be "other-directed" but inner-directed. This reminds me of Saul's story in the bible. The great prophet Samuel had been Saul's connection with God. When Samuel died, Saul's connection with God…died with Samuel.

Now what?

Rather than trying to develop his relationship with God, Saul instead seeks out a medium to call Samuel's spirit from the dead. Saul wants information but does not value having a relationship himself with God, the source of all knowledge. God does not turn away from Saul. Saul turns away from God, as one turns to an adulterous lover. We no doubt glean from the above that Saul failed to build a real relationship with God which is the main reason he still had to go invoke Samuel's spirit from the dead! I mean how dependent on people can one get when we also have the same access to the same God? This is one of the major reasons why seeking and getting to know God for yourself is so crucial.

Read this beautiful article below, written by Thomas A. Tarrants III.

(http://www.cslewisinstitute.org/Knowing_God_Personally_Fu llArticle):

"The Call to Know God

When we speak of knowing God, it is important to understand that we are not talking about abstract or speculative thought concerning God or mystical experiences but about coming alive to God through Jesus Christ and surrendering ourselves to Him in grateful love (Romans 12:1). As John says, "Whoever has the Son has life; whoever does not have the Son of God does not have life" (1 John 5:12).

We must also understand that knowing God is not an optional part of the Christian life; it is the Christian life. Jesus said, "And this is eternal life, that they know you, the only true God, and Jesus Christ whom you have sent" (John 17:3). The English word know in this verse is a translation of the Greek word ginosko, which in this context, means an experiential knowing, not simply an intellectual understanding of facts about God or Jesus or the Bible. In other words, it refers to an "I-Thou" relationship.

This relationship begins when we come alive to God -- that is, when, by grace, we are awakened from the state of spiritual death into which everyone is born, and receive the eternal life Jesus offers to those who trust in Him for salvation. The first part, recognizing and turning from our sins, is repentance; the second part, trusting in Jesus and His atoning death on the cross to forgive our sins, is faith. Coming alive to God requires both. Jesus described this as being born from above or born of the Holy Spirit. It means birth into God's family and entrance into His kingdom (John 3:3–8). **Without rebirth by the Holy Spirit, a person cannot see, perceive, understand, or know God or His kingdom.**

The Call to Go Deeper

As vitally important as the new birth is, that is not the focus of this article. Here I will address what is involved in growing to know God more deeply after the new birth.

The metaphor of birth provides a helpful way of understanding fuller implications of what it means to know God and to grow in that relationship. Just as a human being is physically born into the world and moves through a developmental cycle from infant to child to adolescent to adult, so a child of God is born spiritually and is called to move through a similar developmental cycle. These stages are mentioned in the New Testament. Paul, for example, makes a distinction between "the mature" and "infants in Christ" (1 Cor. 2:6; 3:1), and the writer to the Hebrews does the same (Heb. 5:11–14). John distinguishes between "little children," "fathers," and "young men" (1 John 2:12–14). What does this mean? Spiritually the newest infant in Christ knows God, but not very well. As this baby grows in grace, he or she will progress toward maturity and in doing so will come to know God better and better. We have probably seen this if we have been believers for a while.

What a joy it is to en-counter an infant in Christ, a new convert, eager and zealous for the things of God.

But, what a blessing to meet a father or mother in Christ, a mature believer who has faith-fully walked with God for decades and whose life is characterized by a degree of love, joy, peace, patience, kindness, goodness, faithfulness, gentleness, and self-control that is truly Christ-like! This kind of mature relationship with God is what every believer is called to pursue. As a single lady believing to be joined in union one day it is absolutely okay to get to meet such mature believers and learn some life principles from them and their experience.

The opening chapters of Genesis paint a beautiful picture of Adam and Eve enjoying a personal relationship with God. The story of God and Abraham does the same. But Moses and David open a window into their hunger to know God more intimately. On Mount Sinai, Moses cried out to God, "If I have found favor in your sight, please show me now your ways, that I may know you," and God responded with an extraordinary revelation of Himself (Exodus 33:13; 34:7–9).

Though he was by no means perfect, King David's life (1 & 2 Samuel) and his many psalms reveal a deeply personal relationship with God and a longing for Him: "O God, you are my God; earnestly I seek you; my soul thirsts for you; my flesh faints for you, as in a dry and weary land where there is no water" (Ps. 63:1).

Their hunger for God is an example given to encourage our desire for God (Rom. 15:4).

Knowing God more deeply was not the privilege of only a few luminaries in the Old Testament. God called all of His people to know Him personally and love Him supremely with heartfelt devotion. He called Israel to "love the Lord your God with all your heart and with all your soul and with all your might" (Deut. 6:5). And through Jeremiah, we hear,

Thus says the Lord: "Let not the wise man boast in his wisdom, let not the mighty man boast in his might, let not the rich man boast in his riches, **but let him who boasts boast in this, that he understands and knows me,** that I am the Lord who practices steadfast love, justice, and righteousness in the earth. For in these things I delight, declares the Lord." (Jer. 9:23–24).

God delights when His people truly know Him, love Him, and enjoy the blessings of His faithful love, justice, and righteousness. A notable New Testament example of hunger for God is the apostle Paul. Near the end of his life, Paul said that his greatest passion was "That I may know him and the power of his resurrection, and may share his sufferings" (Phil. 3:10). Paul had had a dramatic encounter with Christ thirty years earlier on the road to Damascus, and he had had several other experiences with Him afterward, but he longed to know Him more deeply. His example shows us that no matter how long or how well we have known the Lord, there is always more.

Paul's longing to know Christ points the way for us as we seek to know God today. We see God most clearly and know Him most nearly through His Son, Jesus Christ. Jesus said, "Whoever has seen me has seen the Father" (John 14:9), and Paul says, "He is the image of the invisible God," and "in him, all the fullness of God was pleased to dwell" (Col. 1:15, 19).

How to Know God More Deeply

Getting to know God more deeply doesn't happen overnight; it takes time. As noted above, Paul had known Christ for many years when he said his passion was to know Christ better. He went on to say, "Not that I have already obtained this or am already perfect, but I press on to make it my own" (Phil. 3:12). Nor is getting to know Christ better an automatic process; it takes real effort. Is effort contrary to grace? No. Grace is opposed to earning (law) but not to effort. Effort is a vital part of how grace operates in sanctification. Thus Paul, the apostle of grace, went on to say to the Philippians:

Not that I have already obtained this or am already perfect, but I press on to make it my own because Christ Jesus has made me His own. Brothers, I do not consider that I have made it my own. But one thing I do: forgetting what lies behind and straining forward to what lies ahead, I press on toward the goal for the prize of the upward call of God in Christ Jesus. Let those of us who are mature think this way, and if in anything you think otherwise, God will reveal that also to you (Phil. 3:12–15).

But (lest we fall into law and self-generated-works righteousness) we must note well, and always remember, that this "straining and pressing on" is not merely unaided human will-power. Rather, it is rooted in the deep work of God in our hearts, arousing hunger and desire and drawing us to engage our wills and strength to seek Him, as Paul had earlier said when he urged the Philippians to "work out your own salvation with fear and trembling, for it is God who works in you, both to will and to work for his good pleasure" (Phil. 2:12–13). Doing this, of course, is utterly dependent upon our being filled with the Holy Spirit daily, for He alone can supply the power we need (which Paul emphasizes in Romans 8, Galatians 5, and Ephesians 5). And the rewards of our Spirit empowered efforts far transcend the greatest earthly pleasures!

Paul's words reinforce the observation that there is a sense in which a person is as close to God as he or she really wants to be. But it is not just Paul who urges us onward. God told Israel, "You will seek me and find me when you seek me with all your heart" (Jer. 29:13). Jesus told His disciples, "Ask, and it will be given to you; seek, and you will find; knock, and it will be opened to you" (Matt. 7:7). In each case, those who seek are the ones who find. And if we don't seek, we will not find.

How do we press on? God offers everything we need in order to grow into deeper fellowship with Him and His Son, but we must embrace it. He gives the milk, but we must drink it. This is what Peter meant when he said, "Like newborn infants, long for the pure spiritual milk, that by it you may grow up into salvation—if indeed you have tasted that the Lord is good" (1 Pet. 2:2–3).

What is the spiritual milk we should long for? Peter is using the image of "newborn infants" to say that just as babies need their mother's milk to grow up physically, so believers need spiritual milk to grow up spiritually. In light of his statements in 1:23–25, it seems very likely that the milk Peter has in mind is the Scriptures, but the way he describes it, he may well mean all the resources necessary for healthy spiritual growth.

The Holy Spirit

Before we look at the essentials that God provides, let's note their source. It is the Holy Spirit, who brings us to new life in Christ in the first place. But that is only the beginning. When Jesus returned to heaven, He handed over to the Holy Spirit His role of teaching, nurturing, strengthening, guiding, and encouraging His followers; the Holy Spirit brings us into union with Christ and is thus called the Spirit of Christ (Rom. 8:9–10). The Spirit now dwells in us and applies in our lives all the benefits that Christ secured for us on the cross: He assures us of forgiveness and salvation, reveals Christ to us in ever-deeper ways, empowers us for holy living, imparts spiritual gifts for ministry and kingdom mission, and guides and directs us to glorify Christ in everything we do — and much more.

Scriptures

What then, are the main sources of spiritual milk that the Spirit gives to mature us in grace and help us know God more intimately? The Holy Scriptures are first. Communication is essential for knowing anyone, including God; and it is primarily through the words of Scripture that God speaks to us. These are God-breathed words that the Holy Spirit inspired holy men of old to record over the centuries, words that the Spirit now illuminates our minds to understand and empowers us to obey. The Scriptures are our only reliable source of knowledge about who God is; what He is like; what His will is; what His plans and purposes are; what He has done in the past; what He will do in the future; who we are; what life is all about; how we can know, love, and serve Him; what are the many promises He gives us; and how we can fulfill His purposes in the world. Accordingly, they are also God's chief instrument for building our faith in Him. The Scriptures are God's ultimate and final authority for what we are to believe and how we are to behave; they are our lifeline in this fallen world.

Prayer

If the Scriptures are God's main way of communicating with us, prayer is our primary way of communicating with Him. It is another essential means for knowing God better. Prayer has been well described as "an offering up of our desires unto God, for things agreeable to His will, in the name of Christ, with confession of our sins, and thankful acknowledgment of His mercies." Often, however, "we do not know what to pray for as we ought," thus we need the Holy Spirit to pray for us and to guide us in our prayers (Rom. 8:26). The Spirit's normal way of guiding us in our prayers is by prompting us through the Scriptures to pray for things that are agreeable to the will of God and will be granted (1 John 5:13–14). This seems to happen more often when we are quietly listening for His word on a particular matter. The Psalms are called "the prayer book of the church," because they give us so many examples of what to pray for across the whole range of life's experiences. And the many promises of God throughout the Bible give us even more. As we walk with God through the ups and downs of life, lifting up our prayers to Him in faith and receiving His answers, our experience with God and our trust in Him grow. And, as the years pass, we develop a history of personal dealings with God that deepens our knowledge of Him, our faith in Him, and our love for Him.

The Church

As vital as Scripture and prayer are, they are not enough. The church is meant to be a vital incubator for growing in the knowledge and love of God. The church was born at Pentecost through the Spirit empowered preaching of the Holy Scriptures. The church is neither a building nor an institutional bureaucracy.

The church is Christ's body on earth, the community of the spiritually reborn, where God is worshiped, His word is faithfully preached, and baptism and the Lord's Supper are properly celebrated.

In the church, the Spirit empowers the preaching of the Scriptures, enlivens our worship and communion with the Father and the Son, deepens our bonds of fellowship with other believers, enables us to care for and minister to one another in love, and sends us out into the world on mission. And much more! This community of Christ is our family. In it, we meet Christ in one another and experience His transforming power together.

Seeking God

Are You Content with your Christian life, or do you long for something more? Do you hunger and thirst for God? Is He the desire of your heart? Do you really want to know Him more intimately and follow Him more faithfully? The pursuit of God is a prerequisite for those who want to go deeper with God. He invites us to seek Him. He shows us the road to travel. And He provides spiritual nourishment for the journey. But these will do us little good unless we make time in our hurried, distracted lives to use them.

Many of us need to take the advice of Dallas Willard: "Hurry is the great enemy of the spiritual life in our day. You must relentlessly eliminate hurry from your life." Jesus was never in a hurry, and we are called to walk in His steps and follow His example. This does not mean withdrawing from normal life and adopting a monastic life. Jesus didn't do that, nor did Moses, David, Peter, or Paul. They led active lives in the world, but their lives were not filled with the clutter, distractions, and chronic busyness that fills our lives today. They were focused, they had priorities, they marched to the beat of a different Drummer; they sought to please an audience of One. No matter where they were or what they were doing, their inner compass was towards God, His presence, His will, and His purposes.

Is that what you long for? If the desire of your heart is to know God more intimately, that is a sign that the grace of God is drawing you. Your part is to respond by setting yourself to seek after and pursue Him (Matthew 6:33). Those who seek will find (Jeremiah 29:13; Matthew 7:7). The following suggestions, drawn from Scripture and demonstrated over many centuries of church history, will be helpful as you seek Him in the days ahead:

• **Worship God** *every Sunday in a church that is orthodox in its beliefs, spiritually alive, and preaches God's word faithfully. Build Christ-centered friendships there, and join a Bible study or prayer group composed of people who want to know God better (Hebrews 10:24). Find a couple of like-minded believers (of your* own gender) and meet regularly to pray and encourage one another in your pursuit of Christ.

• **Read Scripture** daily, asking God to open the eyes of your heart and teach you (Psalm 119:18; 1 Corinthians 2:12; Ephesians 1:16–20). This includes learning to meditate on God's Word and memorize key verses. Meditation takes biblical truth deeper into our minds and hearts with powerful effect. But that effect occurs only as you take to heart what you read and meditate on and become a doer of the word; otherwise, you will not grow spiritually but only become self-deceived (James 1:22–25).

• **Pray daily** in a quiet, undistracted place. If you haven't already done so, learn how to pray the Lord's Prayer, which is the basic prayer Jesus gave to train His disciples. Also, learn to pray other Scriptures. As you read through the Psalms, you will be surprised at how many of them speak directly to your particular needs and concerns today and give you a vocabulary for your own prayer.

• **Ask the Holy Spirit** to fill you each day (Ephesians 5:18); seek to walk in the Spirit (Galatians 5:16) and manifest the fruit of His presence in your life (Galatians 5:22–24). It is impossible to draw near to God or to live the Christian life without the Spirit's help. He reveals Christ to us; He opens our eyes to the Scriptures; He leads us in praying aright; He enlivens our worship; He guides and empowers us for joyful, obedient living and service, and much more. As we walk in the Spirit, we will not fulfill the desires of the flesh (Galatians 5:16).

- **Take time away** to be alone with God when you sense the need. A one day or weekend retreat devoted to seeking God more earnestly about specific concerns can be a source of great blessing or a prayer retreat with one or two friends.

- **Fast periodically.** Jesus said His followers would fast (Matthew 6:16–18; 9:14–15). Fasting and prayer is a way of intensifying our seeking after God and His help, especially in times of personal or national crisis, struggle against sin, spiritual dryness, spiritual warfare, empowerment for ministry, revival of the church, and the advance of God's kingdom. Those who have been closest to God and most fruitful over the centuries have practiced fasting often.

- **Talk with your pastor**/ priest or an elder when you need guidance in your spiritual life. An older, spiritually mature man or woman in the congregation, recommended by the pastor or elders, may also be able to help. This assumes that such a person is well-grounded in Scripture, is humble, manifests the fruit of the Spirit (Galatians 5:22–23), and is wise, godly, and prayerful.

As we seek God and follow Jesus Christ through this fallen world, it will not be easy, "for the gate is narrow and the way is hard that leads to life" (Matthew 7:14). But it is worth it. To be sure, we will experience joys and blessings in our life with God. But arrayed against us is the world, the flesh, and the devil.

So, like Jesus whom we follow, we will meet with hardships and sorrows and encounter "many dangers, toils, and snares." Times of trial and experiences of testing will punctuate our journey. There will be seasons of spiritual dryness; there may be tragedies and perhaps times when God is silent and our prayers seem to go unanswered. We may face persecution. Strong temptations may assail us. But God will be with us and see us through.

He has said, "I will never leave you nor forsake you" (Hebrews 13:5), and He is faithful to sustain us no matter what we encounter. And He will use all the hard things of life (even this waiting period) to help us grow into greater conformity to the image of His Son (Rom. 8:28–29). In the words of a classic hymn "How Firm a Foundation," based on Isaiah 43:1–2, the Lord's promise speaks to us today:

When through the deep waters I call thee to go, The Rivers of
sorrow shall not overflow; for I will be with thee, thy troubles to
bless, and sanctify to thee thy deepest distress. When through
fiery trials thy pathway shall lie, my grace, all-sufficient shall
be all thy supply. The flame shall not hurt thee: I only design,
the dross to consume and thy gold to refine."

EXPLORE, ENGAGE, ENJOY!!!

I CAN'T TALK about singlehood without telling you what such a wonderful phase it is. I believe every phase has its own woes and joys…but as a single lady (with no husband or kids) who understands the temporality of this phase, you have to have all the FUN you can because it's so temporal.

Think of how you sleep wonderfully throughout the night with no intrusion especially having to wake up in the middle of the night to calm a crying baby or breastfeed or change the diapers or make another bottle of milk etc. You rest easy and wake up in the morning refreshed and ready to jet out without having to bathe the kids, dress them up, fix breakfast (listen to their morning complains) and finally get them to school (in an ideal home this task is done and shared amongst the couple to avoid breakdown and wearing one party out).

Now what I just listed is a tip of the iceberg on what the beautiful marriage phase entails. And I really enjoin you to quit the desperation or rush and explore the single-phase, have the most amazing fun and make great use of this time you have alone before the space gets crowded.

In this phase, you can easily pack up your bags to attend impactful conferences without considering if your doctor recommends traveling at this stage (pregnancy) or making plans for who will watch the kids for the few days you will be away. You just have and enjoy this amount of liberty that sometimes some who are married begin to wish the hands of time could be taken backward to give them the privilege to embrace their youthfulness and rock their single phase properly.

In summary, being single could also mean ultimate freedom. This isn't to suggest that being in a relationship is a trap, but it does mean you have to check in with your partner on certain things, share responsibilities, financial and otherwise, and you're simply committed to not just them, but the relationship itself. Commitment to someone you adore completely is wonderful, but sometimes being single is just as wonderful in different ways. Being single doesn't last forever. So instead of worrying about when the next time will be that you'll find yourself on a date with someone who's potentially "The One," enjoy every second of being single. Because when you're in a relationship again, you may very well miss being single.

EXPLORE!

So I said Explore! According to the online *dictionary.cambridge.org*, to explore means: to travel to a new place to learn about it or become familiar with it, to try to discover; learn about something, to search and discover (about something) or to think or talk about something in order to find out more about it. To me, this translates to finding new things to do. It could be new ideas, new cities to explore, new friendships to make, new courses to add to your wealth of knowledge etc. Being married won't stop you from achieving this either, but hey why wait till you are married right?

Learn to develop a passion to explore and learn new things about life. Travel, experience and see life from different plains. Refuse to confine yourself to a particular geographic region (if you don't have to). Learn something new, build new interests, and try new things.

I remember when my interest was to discover and learn new words every day (I still do this, had to subscribe to be part of a particular mailing list that sends new words with their meaning to my email daily.) I come across renowned individuals whose voice matters and are forces to reckon with. I have discovered that they seek to discover, learn and build interest in searching new things. One of such people said in 2018 that learning a new language is the new area of interest to build.

Now, this is how I believe it works; You do not have to go enroll in a school of bilingual studies and pay some fees in other to learn a new language. There a plethora of sites on the internet that gives you the opportunity to enroll in free classes to learn these languages. You can explore new academic fields and add more wealth of knowledge to your knowledge bank. I trained and received my education both degree and masters as a lawyer but the quest to explore and learn more about the human behavior and the workings of the mind drove me to build great interest in psychology. I picked up the habit of reading books on positive psychology and understanding what the concept of happiness really means.

You can check any of these sites for free online courses:

1.   Coursera
2.   edX
3.   Khan Academy
4.   Udemy
5.   iTunesU Free Courses
6.   MIT OpenCourseWare

7.   Stanford Online
8.   Codecademy
9.   Open Culture Online Courses
10.   TED-Ed

It's really not rocket science neither is it necessary to view the single-phase as a curse. Anyone who understands the blessings embedded in this phase will readily make the most impactful use of it.

This brings me to say that marriage actually doesn't make you more "useful" or "purposeful". It only enhances and builds on the goals and visions you represent and wish to fulfill. So, if you have no purpose (explained in the 2nd nugget) or goals in life and if you haven't taken time to understand your purpose for existence, you need to do so, because it is not something "marriage suddenly fixes".

Not to undermine the ache or pressure that comes with the waiting period (in all areas) because as a matter of truth, at times it may seem overwhelming and tough that one really begins to wonder when it will all be over. But flipping the other side of the coin it is trite that if a person gets to the point where they have learned to focus on building and improving themselves (amidst the ache and pressure), they tend to do better and breakthrough more victoriously. It is so because making a decision to not focus on all the things not going well saves you more resourceful energy. It means you are smart enough to not let something you have little or no control over steal your joy, or your ability to be productive, plus your valuable time to be creative and make impact, best of all it means you understand you are not designed to be in total control of how things eventually turn out in the world. Only God is responsible for being in total control.

We all have the impulse to worry over certain issues at one point or the other. However, understanding that over-thinking and constant worries bring little or no positive result, will help bring some sanity to you. This brings the assurance that life works better when we learn to take it one day at a time.

ENJOY!

Take yourself out and treat yourself to the best meals you can afford, stop waiting for someone else to treat you! Growing up in West Africa, Nigeria to be precise. I observed this particular trend during my university days. That outings (lunch or dinner dates, including bills) was something practically left to the 'guys". Some girls prepare to go eat in fast-foods/restaurant with a guy and actually bring their other female friends along (most times without the consent of the young man). I really want to remind you again as stated earlier that no one values you above the value or respect you place on yourself. Having a guy pay for meals is not bad at all, but making it a habit and embracing it as a way of life is not only wrong and myopic but actually shows your level of lack of self- discovery, dependency and entitlement mentality.

And as a general principle of life, 'he who pays the piper dictates the tune' actually applies here. Don't let any Tom Dick and Harry decide what happens because you let them pay the piper, which you have ordinarily paid yourself. Learn to take care of yourself. Say you already have someone (a guy interested in you) and he calls to check up on you, and you respond "oh I am having a cup of ice cream and waiting for my movie time because I am a bit early'...I can bet he understands you aren't waiting for him to buy you one before you can have yourself a cup of ice cream. You must spend your money on yourself, the same way you learn to spend it by investing it in yourself while you wait!!!

Go to church and plan to take yourself on retreats. This gives you time with finding God and finding yourself too.

"You will seek me and find me when you seek me with all your heart." - Jeremiah 29:13

God is always there waiting for us; His arms wide to embrace us but many times we are distracted, looking the other way and missing what he is trying to tell us. While you wait, stay with God and remain in his embrace. Do you want to know why?

"Delight yourself in the Lord and he will give you the desires of your heart." - Psalm 37:4

You could take a day or a few days and go to a secluded spot (hotel, resort or some other place with little or no distractions). Spend time getting to know God again and to know yourself.

Don't isolate yourself or shy away from fun and invitations! Go, have fun and dance well, enjoy yourself, attend your friends' engagements, be merry!!! You must be deliberate and intentional about having a great life while single. I DID, I REALLY DID! And I traveled a lot for conferences when time permitted. Reinvent yourself. In being single, you have a lot of time to figure out who you are, what you want, and in which direction you want to head. If you don't like where you are or who are, change it. It's the perfect time to do so.

Learn to pamper yourself and be unapologetic about it. Part of finding yourself is also making time for you. You have to find time to rest; choose a day to sleep in without any disruptions. Get a pedicure, spa day or buy some nice items that you love. It gives you a chance to learn, love and accept yourself. Just make sure you do what is within your means. A real woman in waiting has no time trying to please or impress anyone. Focus on what matters. Like I always say, not everything matters. Just like all things may be lawful but not all of them are profitable (1 Corinthians 10:23).

Celebrate every success and milestone you hit. And enjoy every single bit of it. You can throw a mini success party. (If you can afford it). Decide to take a driving lesson even if you have not bought a car yet. It's all part of the adventure.

Live, Learn, Read!

Read all you can about this new phase. It has no formula but reading opens you up to other people's experiences, which teaches you a thing or two! SO READ.

ENGAGE!

The few things you can do to engage are listed below. It is more rewarding when we learn to give back to our society. We do not have to be multi-millionaires before we engage or learn to give back. While you wait it can be useful if you find things to do to keep you engaged.

Volunteer With A Charity You Love

It is better to give than to receive. Did you know that giving refreshes the soul? As human beings, most of us want to be part of something greater than us. Something that makes a difference. This hunger is not always for positive things but we can channel it for good.

There are so many charities, NGO's and social initiatives out there, doing good works and making a difference. Consider volunteering your time and resources. This could be on a temporary or permanent basis - You choose.

Find something that resonates with you; It could be around **domestic violence, sexual abuse, child trafficking, refugees, addictions, animals** or even the environment.

Get Involve In Your Community

You may be wondering how this is different from volunteering. Beyond volunteering with a charity, there are things you could also do within your community (for undergraduate students join organizations that help build you up). You could promote social activities, join the associations and help them implement changes that will improve your community and livelihoods.

Imagine how much fun it could be coming up with activities and helpful changes in your neighborhood. This will shift your focus to something bigger than yourself and you will definitely be better for it.

Conclusion

LIFE THEY SAY is not a bed of roses, and although roses are beautiful, they have their own thorns. We all go through life having different experiences and learning from them as well. The whole essence of the nuggets shared in this book is to let you know how much power you have and why you need to build yourself properly before you get married to your "prince charming". No one ever regrets the time they invested in themselves or the impacts they made or how much they positively affected other people. Thus it should be your priority to make your life count irrespective of what status or title you are bearing at the moment.

You are a masterpiece, God's precious one and as cornerstones, polished after the similitude of a palace. Your worth is priceless and far above rubies. At some point in life, we all have to wait for certain things. The reason often times we may not understand but Scripture makes us understand that everything works together for our good. This knowledge like I said earlier calms the heart because even subconsciously we accept the truth that no matter how rough it is or how overwhelming the journey is, there is good coming out from it eventually.

God knows about the wait, He has it all planned out (before I formed you I knew you). Not having received what you've been waiting for till now does not mean he has forgotten. He lives in eternity, therefore, He is not subject to our time limitations and setbacks. Your duty is to make the best use of the waiting period. Become the best you can be, do the best you can and produce the best version of you (believe me this will save you tons of stress when the wait is over).

Be confident that when the wait is over you will make the most amazing wife. Build yourself and develop till you understand how much of an asset you are, not just to the man but the nation at large. No man does you a favor by marrying you. Over time people in the society have made this look like the norm. However, you must understand you are the embodiment of favor and "good thing", thus Scriptures reference to finding a wife as "finding something good and obtaining favor from the Lord".

Know your value and worth and do not be apologetic in enforcing the right standards. You may be criticized but that is okay, do not let your heart be troubled, Jesus too was criticized (I bet you maintaining certain standards comes with its own criticisms). Be the kind of woman who will refuse to settle for less.

You have been designed in God's image and likeness. You have equally been given the mind of Christ. Also, the same spirit that raised Jesus from death lives on the inside of you! You cannot possess all these qualities and yet let yourself be trampled upon like someone with no purpose or direction. I know "the wait" may be rough and uneasy especially with the fact that sometimes we have our "emotions" to deal with. But I just want you to use the waiting period to focus on building and developing you. Never let yourself be deceived into thinking that someone promising to marry you tantamount to doing you a favor. No, you are the one bringing the favor and good so you must carry yourself with some degree of respect.

Be deliberate and intentional about making your standards known and never let anyone subdue you or manipulate you to compromise. You may have heard it before that "if he loves you, he will wait". This is true because this saying became my reality. I made my standards known and stood by it. Men most times will cajole you to compromise when they see you aren't firm or persistent on what you profess. I charge you to take charge of your singlehood, make the best of it and hold strongly to the right standards you have set. Never allow yourself to think thoughts that limit you or make you feel less. Again, do not be ashamed of being single. There is power in refusing to settle for someone who doesn't truly deserve you. Always remember you are smart, special, beautiful, graced, and intelligent, a force to reckon with, a trailblazer, a battle axe in Gods' hand, a powerful woman created to impact and bless her generation.

Positive Affirmation

If you're single and want a loving, caring relationship someday, then it can be a struggle sometimes. This is especially true if you talk negatively about being single. You may not like being single, but if you say things like 'I hate being single!' then you are setting yourself up for some bad stuff.

For instance, you can lower your standards as you become desperate for a relationship and end up getting into a relationship that drags you down and makes you miserable. That's why you need to talk to yourself in a way that helps you maintain your standards (and your sanity) as you look for that special someone. *There are people out there who are waiting to meet you, waiting to love you. You have to stick around for them.*

Learn to use affirmations when acknowledging or speaking to yourself. Below are some examples of affirmations you can practice with (go-ahead to create yours).

- **I Deserve A Good Person In My Life:** First and foremost, you need to believe that you deserve a good person in your life.

- **I Enjoy Having Time To Do Whatever I Want:** You are single! You make your own decisions with your time. You can sit on the couch all day and do nothing or you can take courses, work on yourself, or take trips whenever you want to. You don't have to answer to anyone. If you want to do it, you can do it. A person has to spend some quality time being themselves on their own terms without distractions. It helps you get to know yourself, see your potential, and build a foundation of who you will be for the rest of your life.

- **I'm Happy for People Who Have Found True Love:** If you hate on couples that are really happy, you are going to torture yourself needlessly. You will start saying things to yourself like 'That's what I'm missing out on!' And the more you tell yourself that you are missing out on something great, the more horrible you will feel because you will feel like you are missing something big from your life! That's painful and it will make any single person miserable. If they are happy, that's something you should celebrate, not hate on. When you feel happy for them, you maintain your own personal happiness. Your focus stays on how good relationships can be, and you can maintain a positive expectation that one day you will be in a relationship like that.

•   **There's more to Life than Relationships:** In other words, you are constantly working on improving yourself and achieving a happier and healthier life. And a relationship is just one of those areas. You also have family and friends, spirituality, career, finances, fun, contribution, health, physical environment, and personal development to focus on. So why give all your attention to a relationship – or lack thereof, when it is just a fraction of what makes up your well-being and happiness in life? There is so much more to life than relationships, and they don't require you to be in a relationship to work on them.

•   **My Relationship Status Doesn't Define Me:** Before it was just our mothers and nosy people who worried about our relationship status. That was bad enough. But now we have to disclose our relationship status on social media where we think everyone can judge us based on it. But that's crap. While I'm sure some people may judge you on your relationship status (because they are emotionally unintelligent people who do things like that), most people base their opinion of you on more things than whether you are single or not. But whether they are judging you or not, you must remember that there's more to life than relationships and your relationship status doesn't define you and what kind of life you have. There are so many more elements of your life that define what kind of person you are and what kind of person you are going to be.

- **I Am Lovable:** I don't need to know you, I already know that there is a lot to love about you. You have unique qualities that would enrich other people's lives. You are a human being and deserve love. You have done good things for people. You have a lot to offer someone in a relationship. And, if you don't truly believe you are lovable, yet, saying this affirmation over and over again will help you look for those little things that make you so lovable. You will even find yourself creating more things about yourself that makes you appealing and a good catch.

Finally, I want to charge you to declare to yourself boldly saying: *"I will be the best I can while I wait through Christ who strengthens me and when the wait is over I will be a strong fulfilled purposeful woman because he is indeed blessed that finds me."*

Works Cited

1) https://www.dictionary.com/browse/discover

2) https://www.theodysseyonline.com/guide-to-finding-yourself

3)https://dgreatinfluencer.blogspot.com/2019/03/hello-fear_54.html?m=1

4)http://www.cslewisinstitute.org/Knowing_God_Personally_Full Article

5) Benedict Smith,
https://positiveaffirmations101.com/affirmations-single-people-will-benefit-from/

www.ingramcontent.com/pod-product-compliance
Lightning Source LLC
Chambersburg PA
CBHW061252140726

47998CB00006B/2203